THE
FLEET AIR ARM
IN FOCUS

PART ONE

PRICE £6.95

For Jandy & Andrew who typed, helped and encouraged

This is not a history but an attempt to capture something of the spirit of the Fleet Air Arm through a collection of photographs put together over a number of years. My grateful thanks go to Brian Beer, Geoffrey David, Bob Duke, John Hayman, Antony Pearce and all the others who have contributed photographs. My especial thanks to Len Lovell (until recently on the staff of the Fleet Air Arm Museum) for his encouragement and assistance. A special thank you must also go to Lt Cdr Larcombe RN of the Fleet Photographic Unit who allowed me to make use of some of his rarer pictures.

HMS HERMES was a HIGHFLYER class Cruiser completed in 1899. In 1913 she was converted to become a depot ship for the Royal Naval Air Service. A launching platform was built over the forecastle and a canvas hangar for two seaplanes was erected aft. The trials she carried out with the fleet during 1913 were so successful that they led the Admiralty to order the new ARK ROYAL specifically to carry aircraft. HERMES is seen here sinking shortly after having been torpedoed by U27 off Ruylingen Bank on 31 October 1914. The remains of the hangar and a damaged seaplane are visible on the quarterdeck.

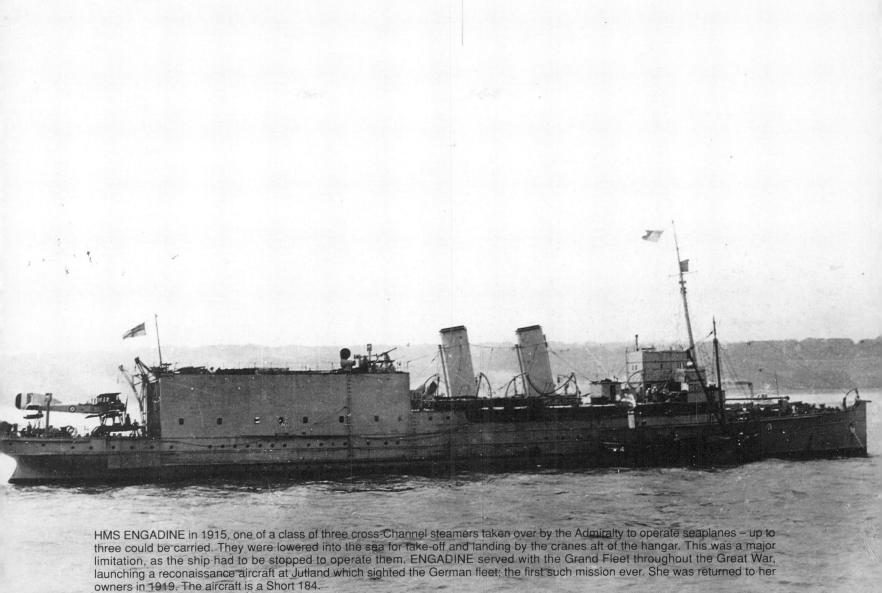

HMS ENGADINE in 1915, one of a class of three cross-Channel steamers taken over by the Admiralty to operate seaplanes – up to three could be carried. They were lowered into the sea for take-off and landing by the cranes aft of the hangar. This was a major limitation, as the ship had to be stopped to operate them. ENGADINE served with the Grand Fleet throughout the Great War, launching a reconaissance aircraft at Jutland which sighted the German fleet; the first such mission ever. She was returned to her owners in 1919. The aircraft is a Short 184.

Flying trials carried out on HMS FURIOUS in May 1918 to test the after landing deck. The aircraft is a Sopwith PUP modified with a skid type undercarriage rather than the normal wheels. The fore and aft wires were intended to hold the aircraft firmly on deck after landing in gusty and turbulent wind conditions, by means of engaging hooks fitted onto the skid axle. The vertical ropes visible in the foreground formed part of a barrier rigged to prevent any aircraft that overshot from crashing into the funnel.

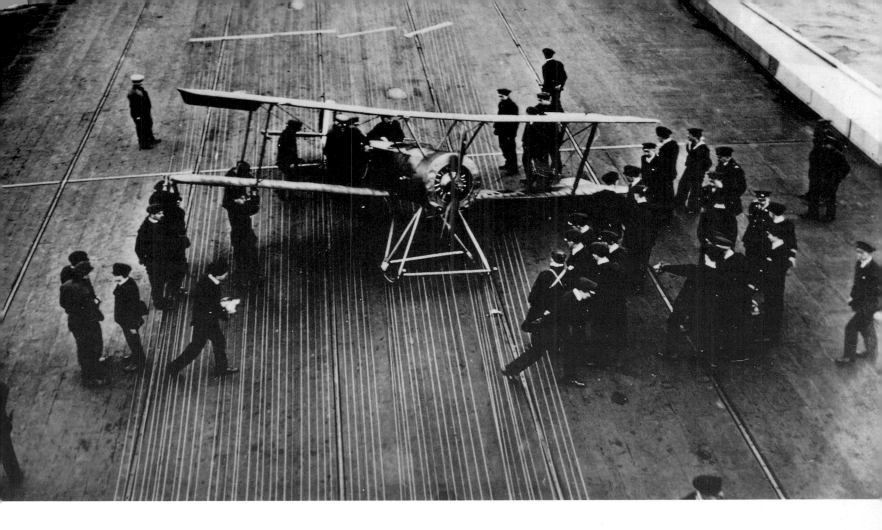

The majority of attempts to land on HMS FURIOUS resulted in failure and crashes like this one. The bridge and funnel had been left on the centreline between the two flight decks. The considerable turbulence they caused was too much for the light aircraft of the day which became uncontrollable close to the deck. Note that the wires have held the aircraft on deck but may have added to its damage. Visible aft of the Sopwith PUP are flat planks intended to keep the wires off the deck like the bridge under violin strings. They have been knocked flat as the aircraft passed them helping to slow it – but contributing to the punishment it has taken!

HMS ARK ROYAL (2) in December 1918. She was the first ship in the Royal Navy built specifically to carry and operate seaplanes. The decision to build her was taken after the successful HERMES trials of 1913 but to speed completion the incomplete hull of a tramp steamer already under construction was used.

HMS FURIOUS in 1918 with Sopwith 2F1 Camels on her flying off deck. Aft of the aircraft, in the foreground is the hatch through which they were moved from and to the hangar by derrick. The posts around the deck acted as a windbreak and safety barrier. They were lowered for flying operations.

HMS ARGUS in 1918 with her original dazzle paint scheme. She was the first ship in the world to be completed as an aircraft carrier in the modern sense. Again, an incomplete merchant ship hull formed the basis of the ship in order to minimise delay – in this case a liner originally to have been named CONTE ROSSO for the Italian Lloyd Sabudo Line.

HMS ARGUS after World War 1 but still largely as built. W/T masts and the charthouse are raised into the non-flying position. The ship is at anchor with a steam pinnace alongside. Just visible aft is smoke issuing from the funnel tubes which ran along between the hangar roof and the flight deck. This complicated arrangement was never very successful and was not repeated in later carriers. Note how the flight deck is a separate structure held above the hull by lattice girders. The aircraft on deck is a Sopwith PUP.

HMS EAGLE in China Station paint scheme seen sailing from Plymouth Sound in 1933. She was originally laid down as the battleship ALMIRANTE COCHRANE for Chile but was purchased by the Admiralty and became another first world war conversion. The original battleship hull is still quite evident; a sister ship, HMS CANADA, served as a battleship during the first world war. Note the large crane at the after end of the island intended for operating seaplanes and the pronounced 'hump' at the after part of the flight deck intended to give a smooth airflow over the landing area.

HMS HERMES in November 1934. Although originally conceived as a seaplane carrier, she was the first in the world to be laid down and built as a carrier. Like EAGLE she has a large crane to work seaplanes and an aerodynamic hump aft.

HMS GLORIOUS in 1935. The short "flying off deck" forward was intended to allow fighters to launch out of the upper hangar directly over the bows – even if the main flight deck was unusuable. It fell into disuse in the 1930s when aircraft weights increased to the point where they needed a longer run to get airborne. She could be told apart from her sister COURAGEOUS by the longer flight deck aft supported by an arrangement of struts in a 'W' shape. W/T masts are raised in the non-flying position and divisions are fallen in on the flight deck.

Another view of GLORIOUS. The fence like structures aft of the island are palisades intended to prevent an aircraft that landed off-centre from being blown over the side. By this stage aircraft were arrested by modern athwartships wires which engaged a hook fitted to the aircraft. Seaplanes could be brought through doors from the lower hangar onto the quarterdeck and operated by the cranes seen folded away under the flight deck. Note the platform structure visible to port of the funnel. This was intended to give Commander Flying an optimum view of aircraft operations on the flight deck and was the forerunner of the modern Flyco. It was hinged and could be pulled back flush with the island side when not needed. Divisions are clearly over and the men dispersing.

The hinged flying control position can be seen to better advantage in this view of GLORIOUS. The doors which led from the upper hangar onto the forward flight deck are open, topped by the pronounced curved leading edge of the upper flight deck. This was intended to give a smooth airflow over the deck but by 1935 it was modified by the two block like structures that housed the hydraulic catapult mechanisms.

HMS COURAGEOUS shows her shorter flight deck aft. Her seaplane handling arrangements identical to those in GLORIOUS can also be seen. The requirement for carriers to operate seaplanes was only dropped during World War 2. The downward curve at the after part of the flight deck is called a round down and served to lessen the risk of a crash if a pilot came too low over the stern.

HM Submarine M2 secured alongside. She was originally completed in 1918 with an armament of 4x18" torpedo tubes and a 12" 40 calibre gun forward of the conning-tower. In 1928, she was extensively modified with a hangar and catapult in place of the gun. The aircraft is a Parnall PETO, designed specially for this task and built of stainless steel to minimise the effects of corrosion. The pilot and observer drew special service pay for both flying and submarines, something not many have been able to do over the years! M2 foundered off Portland in January 1932.

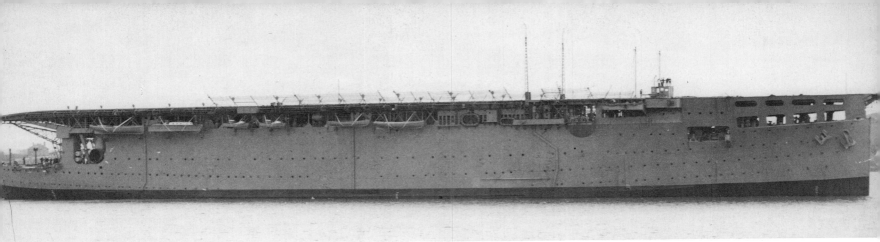

HMS ARGUS after conversion to a training carrier and QUEEN BEE drone target operating ship in November 1938. The flight deck forward is more heavily plated in order to support the weight of a hydraulic catapult. Palisades are fitted to port and starboard of the landing area. The ship is not at flying stations and has the charthouse and W/T masts raised. She is underway in pilotage waters (note the starboard anchor ready for letting go) and is being conned from the charthouse roof.

HMS ARGUS in dry dock at Hebburn-on-Tyne after her reconstruction. The substantial new structure supporting the catapult is more evident in this view.

HMS ARK ROYAL (3) anchored off Spithead on 16 June 1939. This famous ship was the culmination of many years of design work between the wars and represented a very great step forward from the prototypes and conversions that served before her. As always, great emphasis was placed on aerodynamic efficiency; note the rounded shape of the flight deck forward with the catapult structures evident on either side of it. W/T masts are raised as is the port crane jib. The can shaped object at the masthead is a Type 72 aircraft homing beacon.

Another view of ARK ROYAL (3) showing the enormous overhang aft. This was not intended to lengthen the deck for aircraft use but rather to give the optimum airflow in the landing area. The failure of the early landing experiments in FURIOUS clearly made the deepest impression on British designers! Whilst ARK ROYAL did not have an armoured hangar like later fleet carriers, the hull was protected to cruiser standards and the armoured belt is visible here forward of the accommodation ladder. Note that the multiple pom-poms and heavy machine guns have not yet been fitted.

HMS ÍLLUSTRIOUS shortly after her completion in 1940. Unlike any previous carrier she had an armoured flight deck and the hangar beneath it was an armoured box. Because of the weight this involved, there was only room for one hangar and thus only half the number of aircraft possible in ARK ROYAL (3) could be carried. Again, considerable emphasis was placed on smooth airflow over the deck and pronounced round-downs were built fore and aft. These reduced the usable flight deck by 120 feet and later in the war they were flattened out to enable more aircraft to be operated.

A quarter view of ILLUSTRIOUS in Plymouth Sound (June 1940). All W/T masts and cranes are in the raised, non-flying position. The new style 4.5" gun turrets are mounted high to enable them to fire across the flight deck and indeed the port after mounting can be seen trained to starboard. A hastily fitted de-gaussing loop can be seen externally at quarterdeck level.

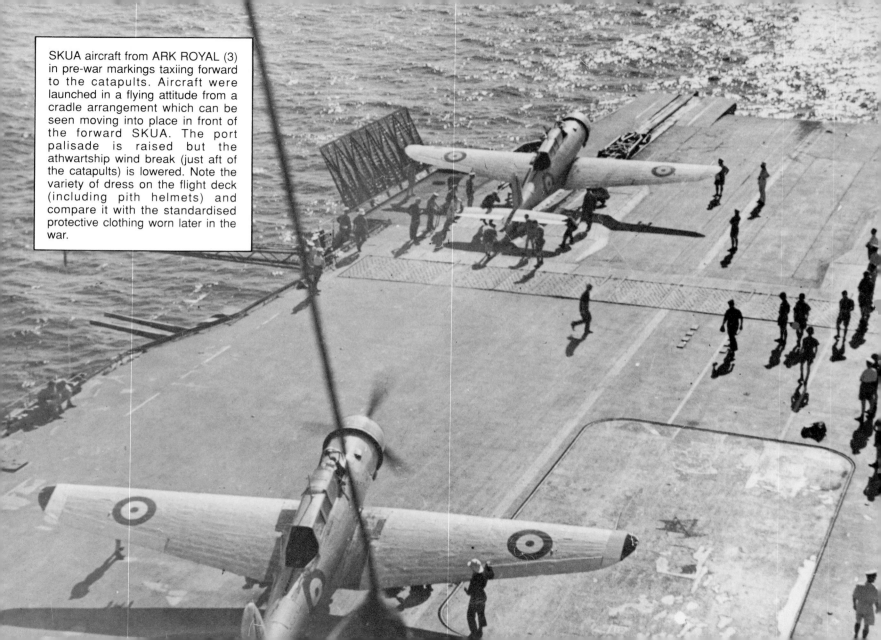

SKUA aircraft from ARK ROYAL (3) in pre-war markings taxiing forward to the catapults. Aircraft were launched in a flying attitude from a cradle arrangement which can be seen moving into place in front of the forward SKUA. The port palisade is raised but the athwartship wind break (just aft of the catapults) is lowered. Note the variety of dress on the flight deck (including pith helmets) and compare it with the standardised protective clothing worn later in the war.

SKUAS of 801 and 803 Squadrons lined up ready for take off from ARK ROYAL (3). They are in early wartime camouflage. From the expectant look on the chock-men's faces and the slight tilt on the deck, the ship is turning into wind and about to start the launch. The chock-man on the starboard wheel of the first aircraft is probably a new hand and has a more experienced rating at his shoulder to make sure that he does the job properly. There are a number of bombs stowed aft of the wooden pontoon on deck but none have had their tails or fuzes fitted. Even so, it does seem surprising to see that the right hand officer sitting on the pontoon is smoking a pipe! (As is at least one of the group in the foreground). With both highly volatile AVGAS and ammunition in close proximity, smoking would not be tolerated today.

SWORDFISH disembarked at RNAS HATSTON (1942) near Kirkwall in the Orkneys (the spire of St Magnus Cathedral is visible in the distance). Some aircraft are already armed and others being armed with 18" torpedoes. SKUAs are visible in the distant dispersals.

HMS FURIOUS in her final guise. The original 5.5" anti-surface guns have been replaced by twin 4" Mark 19 mountings. A small island has been built conventionally to starboard with a mast to support the Type 72 homing beacon. Although for the most part camouflaged, the after part of the ship is painted black to mask smoke staining. She is not at flying stations here, the W/T masts are raised and smoke is being exhausted through the holes in the flight deck aft, a process known as "smoking up".

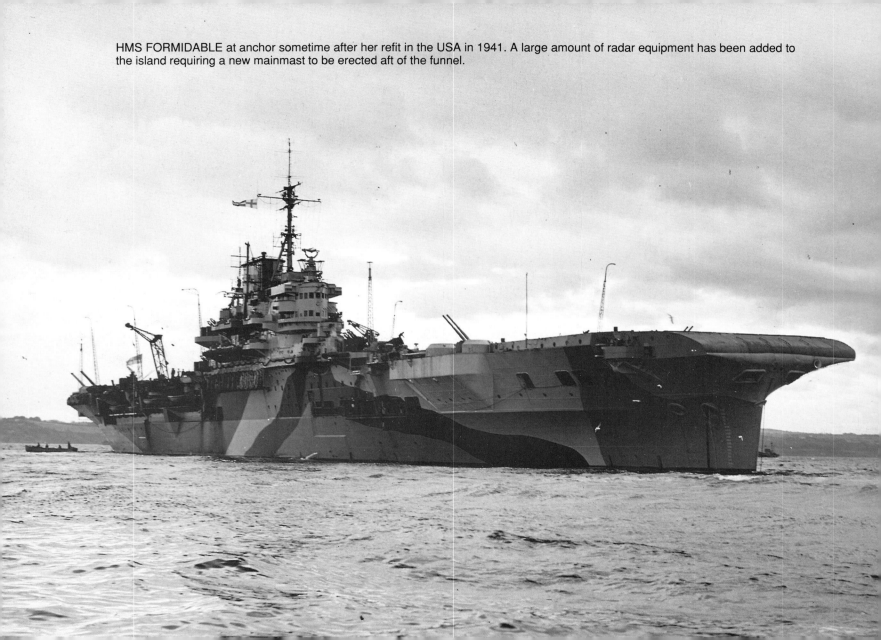

HMS FORMIDABLE at anchor sometime after her refit in the USA in 1941. A large amount of radar equipment has been added to the island requiring a new mainmast to be erected aft of the funnel.

HMS FORMIDABLE viewed from aft. Extra 20mm anti-aircraft guns have been added and the new lattice mast supports a VHF aircraft homing device which, unlike the W/T masts raised in this picture, could not be lowered. Visible on the after round-down are three outriggers fitted to enable aircraft to be pushed as far aft as possible on deck when ranged, their tail wheels slotting into the outrigger. They are a very good idea but make it a little difficult for the pilot to do his walk-round checks before start-up! The introduction of nosewheel undercarriages post war made it easier to park aircraft with their tails over the side of the ship thus getting more on deck.

HMS ARCHER was the first American built escort carrier to enter service with the Royal Navy. She was converted from the mercantile MORMACLAND by the Newport News Shipbuilding Company in November 1941. The small hangar is clearly visible aft as is the structure forward of it supporting the 438 foot flight deck. A small island can just be seen on the starboard side with British radar equipment installed on it.

A SWORDFISH floatplane being lowered over the side of a cruiser prior to take-off from the water. A steadying rope is looped through a special rail under the aircraft rudder, it will be pulled clear when the aircraft is safely in the water. The officer with the flag is giving directions to the crane driver.

The ship's company abandon HMS ARK ROYAL (3) after she was hit by a torpedo from U81 east of Gibraltar on 13 November 1941. She had just recovered aircraft when she received the single hit on the starboard side, amidships; the W/T masts are thus in the lowered, flying position. The external degaussing cable is prominent.

Another HMS ENGADINE saw service in World War 2. Like her predecessor she was a converted merchant ship intended to operate seaplanes. In the event, she and her sister ship were used as aircraft transports able to carry about 20 folded aircraft in the hangars and holds or about 40 dismantled aircraft stowed more densely. The heavy duty cranes visible fore and aft were intended to work seaplanes but proved useful for loading and unloading aircraft.

HMS FENCER in 1943 shortly after delivery to the Royal Navy under Lend/Lease arrangements. She is altogether a better conversion than ARCHER with a larger hangar and two lifts instead of one.

An officer makes adjustments to the fuze of a torpedo fitted to a SWORDFISH on HMS BATTLER whilst the pilot looks on. There is no sense of urgency and the picture is clearly posed for a wartime press release. BATTLER, like FENCER was an American built escort carrier of the ATTACKER class. Clearly such ships were delivered equipped to the last detail as most of those visible are wearing American steel helmets! Note the wooden flight deck, a feature found only in American carriers.

The original wartime caption reads "A naval pilot running to his HURRICANE which stands ready and bombed up on the airfield." When HMS FORMIDABLE was heavily damaged, she withdrew from the Mediterranean disembarking her squadrons to form part of 201 Naval Co-operation Group of the Middle East Air Force. After the drive into Syria, the two Naval Fighter Squadrons, 803 and 806 were re-armed with ex-RAF HURRICANES to form the Naval Fighter Wing which flew extensively in support of the Army in North Africa. Again the infinite variety of service dress is worthy of note.

ALBACORES ranged ready for launch from a fleet carrier in about 1941. The aircraft are unarmed and there is no sense of urgency, so notwithstanding the size of the launch, it is probably for practice during a work-up. The ALBACORE was designed to be a maid-of-all-work, note the variety of torpedo and bomb crutches under wing and fuselage. The objects like TV aerials on the aircraft nearest the camera are ASV radar antennae.

HMS VICTORIOUS refuels from a US Navy oiler whilst serving with the American Pacific Fleet in 1943. She embarked three fighter squadrons 882, 896 and 898 equipped with WILDCATS and a strike squadron, 832, equipped with AVENGERS. VICTORIOUS and her air group used USN doctrine and tactics and, as can be seen, the aircraft even sported US style star markings.

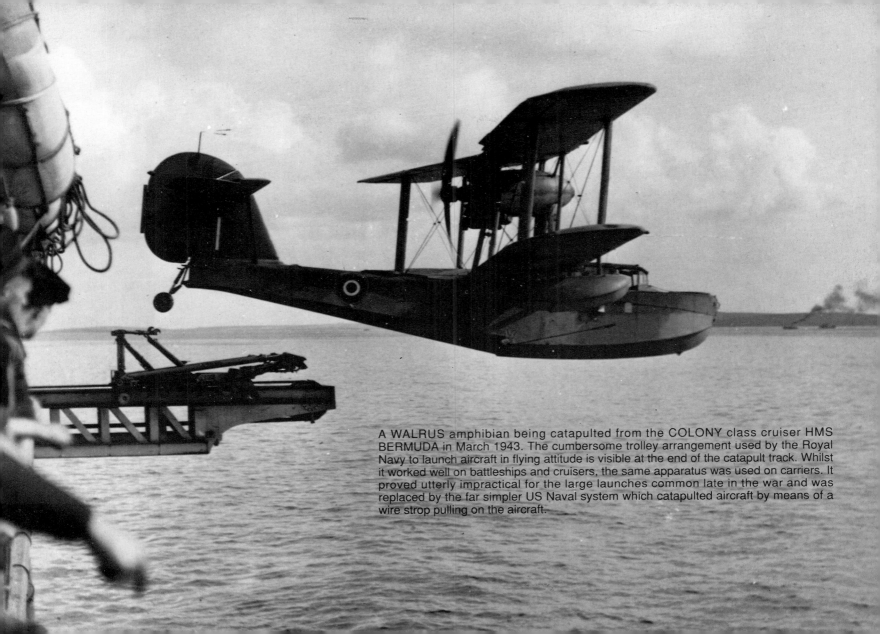

A WALRUS amphibian being catapulted from the COLONY class cruiser HMS BERMUDA in March 1943. The cumbersome trolley arrangement used by the Royal Navy to launch aircraft in flying attitude is visible at the end of the catapult track. Whilst it worked well on battleships and cruisers, the same apparatus was used on carriers. It proved utterly impractical for the large launches common late in the war and was replaced by the far simpler US Naval system which catapulted aircraft by means of a wire strop pulling on the aircraft.

An early production BARRACUDA II Torpedo Bomber Reconnaissance aircraft. Note the huge bay windows under the wing intended to give the observer the best possible view. The torpedo is an 18" Mark VIII and is fitted with a wooden monoplane air tail (MAT) intended to improve the weapon's flight in air. This allowed it to be launched higher and faster in order to reduce the time an aircraft would be under fire during an attack.

A SEA HURRICANE fighter taking off from HMS AVENGER whilst she works up for service with the Home Fleet in July 1942. Formerly the merchant ship RIO HUDSON, she was one of the early American escort carrier conversions and was accepted by the Royal Navy on 2 March 1942. She served mainly on convoy escort duties before being lost off Gibraltar on 15 November 1942 when a torpedo from U155 detonated in the bomb room which then exploded. She broke up and sank within 3 minutes.

HMS PEGASUS (formerly ARK ROYAL (2)). In 1930 she was commissioned as a catapult trials ship, testing new equipment for use in battleships and cruisers. She was renamed PEGASUS in 1934 to free the more famous name for use by the planned new fleet carrier. She saw brief active service during 1941-42 when she was used as a fighter catapult ship to provide desperately needed convoy air defence until the new escort carriers became available in quantity. She was relegated to duty as an accommodation ship in 1944 and, surprisingly in view of her age, sold for merchant use in 1947.

HMS SEARCHER with WILDCAT fighters of 882 and 898 Squadrons on deck. She was commissioned into the Royal Navy at Portland, Oregon on her completion on 7 April 1943 and served as a fighter carrier with the Home Fleet until 1945. She took part in a number of strikes in Norwegian waters including Operation TUNGSTEN, the attack on the TIRPITZ. After a brief spell with the East Indies Fleet, she was returned to the US Navy at Norfolk, Virginia in November 1945.

The tanker RAPANA seen after conversion into a Merchant Aircraft Carrier (MAC-Ship). Both bulk grain and oil tankers were converted to operate flights of 4 SWORDFISH aircraft. MAC-Ships flew the red ensign and had merchant crews with a naval detachment to operate the aircraft. They retained most of their cargo carrying capacity. The tankers had no hangar and hence no lift, the aircraft remaining on deck in all weathers. The Swordfish came from 836 Squadron and on some of them, the words ROYAL NAVY were unofficially painted out by their crews and replaced by MERCHANT NAVY.

HMS EMPRESS was a Lend/Lease escort carrier which was built as such at Seattle rather than converted from a merchant hull. She was commissioned by the Royal Navy in Vancouver, British Columbia on 12 August 1943 and fitted out as an assault carrier in order to operate fighter-bomber type aircraft. She served with Western Approaches Command until late 1944 when she was refitted on the Clyde for service with the East Indies Fleet. She is seen here on 16 December 1944 when that work was completed. She was returned to the USN on 4 February 1946 and broken up.

HMS NABOB, a SMITER class escort carrier commissioned at Seattle on 7 September 1943. She was manned by the Royal Canadian Navy – with the exception of the Air Department – but remained a unit of the Royal Navy. She is seen after being hit and damaged by a torpedo from U354 on 22 August 1944 which blew a hole 50 feet by 40 feet below the waterline and bent the propeller shaft. Once back in Scapa Flow she was deemed to be too badly damaged to warrant repair and was reduced to reserve. After the war she was repaired and sold for merchant service and was not finally broken up until 1977.

HMS ATTACKER in January 1943, four months after commissioning. She saw extensive service as an assault carrier, including the invasions of North Africa and Southern France. She served with the 21st Aircraft Carrier Squadron in the East Indies Fleet during 1945 with SEAFIRES of 879 Squadron embarked. Note the wooden flight deck and single catapult to port of the forward lift. She was returned to the USN at Norfolk, Virginia on 5 January 1946 and converted for merchant service. She ended her days as a floating hotel in the Phillipines, until being broken up in 1980.

HMS ARBITER was commissioned on 31 December 1943 in Portland, Oregon but did not arrive in the UK until June 1944. After brief service with Western Approaches Command she joined the British Pacific Fleet in early 1945 for service as a Ferry Carrier. She is seen here in the Admiralty Light paint scheme used from 1944 onwards.

A Grumman HELLCAT Mark I fighter, a USN type supplied to the Royal Navy under Lend/Lease arrangements. This mark was des-
ignated the F6F-3 in the USN and there were 130 aircraft in this particular delivery. At first, the aircraft was re-named the GANNET
in British service but the name never proved popular and the American name was substituted in 1944. The markings are those
applied to all naval aircraft west of Suez from March 1942 onwards.

The Fairey SWORDFISH adapted remarkably well to a number of roles. They outlived the ALBA-CORE which was intended to replace it both in production and service. These are Mark IIs from a batch of 350 built by Blackburn (known colloquially as "BLACKFISH"). They are sporting black and white D-Day invasion recognition stripes. Rails for 60lb rockets are fitted underwing and the under-wing skins are metal rather than fabric – to avoid scorching from the rockets when fired.

A CORSAIR fighter has crashed into the barrier of a fleet carrier and suffered major damage. The initial panic is over, hoses have been run out and the immediate risk of fire has been averted. Note the two firesuitmen to the left of the aircraft behind the broken off wing and the handlers running forward with extra fire extinguishers. Jumbo, the flight deck crane, has been started up and is moving in to clear the wreckage; other aircraft may be waiting to land on and it is important that the deck is cleared for them as soon as possible. The aircraft forward is a half folded BARRACUDA.

Aircraft on HMS VICTORIOUS ranged for a major Home Fleet strike in 1944. Those forward are CORSAIRS, those aft are BARRACUDAS. Note how much better flight deck dress has become with wind-proof gabardine overalls, coloured surcoats for directors and helmets.

A CORSAIR Mark II has missed all the arrester wires, hit the first barrier high and flipped onto its back over the second barrier. This aircraft was one of a batch of 605 delivered via Blackburn who carried out modifications for the Royal Navy. Two firesuitmen in their 'Fearnought' suits stand by in case of fire whilst the handling teams work out how to clear the wreckage from the flight deck.

Another CORSAIR caught cartwheeling after missing all the wires and catching the barrier high. The markings are those worn by the East Indies Fleet with small roundels omitting any red to avoid confusion with Japanese 'rising sun' markings. T indicates the parent carrier, HMS VICTORIOUS; 8 indicates 1836 Squadron, and G the individual aircraft.

A SEAFIRE Mark III crashing into the forward barrier of a fleet carrier. The propeller blades are breaking up with pieces flying in all directions, a very real danger to flight deck personnel. A long range fuel tank is fitted between the oleos.

A CORSAIR in Eastern Fleet markings has crashed into the after barrier of a fleet carrier, demolishing it. It has come to rest at the base of the island by the starboard stanchion of the forward barrier. The starboard wing has been torn off and fire has already broken out in the engine bay area and in the starboard wing stub. An aircraft handler is running in by the port wingtip with foam firefighting equipment.

Foam is sprayed onto the wreck to cut down the flames.

The fire is out; slings have been attached to the aircraft so that Jumbo the Crane can lift it clear. It will probably be stripped of anything serviceable and thrown over the side. An engineer officer and several mechanics in their shorts have come up from the hangar to help strip the wreck as time could well be limited.

Jumbo lifts the wreck clear while handlers hose down and clean the deck.

Sod's Opera, HMS ARBITER at Manus, 1945. The aircraft lifts and the large open space in the hangar are ideal for amateur variety shows such as this one.

Deck hockey, HMS ARBITER 1945. Carriers may change in appearance but the popularity of this sport has never wavered.

HMS UNICORN, designed as a maintenance carrier and completed in 1943. As well as double hangars and elaborate workshops, she had full flying facilities and was used as an operational carrier briefly. If they could not be flown on, aircraft could be brought to the ship by means of a special lighter stowed, when not in use, under an overhang at the after end of the flight deck. She served during the war with the Mediterranean, East Indies and British Pacific Fleets. Post war she was used as a ferry and support carrier for the Commonwealth carriers off Korea before being broken up in 1959.

BARRACUDAS of the East Indies Fleet carrying out a strike operation during 1944. The picture is taken through the observer's bay window of a Barracuda and includes a 250lb bomb under that aircraft's port wing in the foreground. The bomb is tail fused in order to detonate after impact rather than on contact; the vane visible at the rear of the bomb is designed to spin in the slipstream whilst falling, arming the bomb after a set number of turns.

Folded on deck, the BARRACUDA looked like the result of an accident. In flight though it could be graceful as this posed picture of a Mark II shows.

A HELLCAT, 5A, the Commanding Officer of 1839 Squadron's aircraft goes over the side of HMS INDOMITABLE in 1944. The forward barrier is up and has not been hit but the propellers show signs of damage and the engine has stopped. The pilot has probably lined up too far to the left and struck the deck edge before his momentum carried the aircraft over the side

HMS FORMIDABLE hit by a Kamikaze on 4 May 1945. A number of aircraft were airborne at the time and so only eleven were lost on deck. The fires have been put out and work is starting on clearing the wreckage in order to get the ship back into action. Splinters had damaged the centre boiler room and the armoured flight deck was dented but repaired with quick drying cement. The ship was fully back in action by sunset.

HMS COLOSSUS serving with the British Pacific Fleet in September 1945 with CORSAIRS of 1846 Squadron and BARRACUDAS of 827 Squadron embarked. She was the first of the Light Fleet Carriers to complete on 16 December 1944 but only served for a short while in the Royal Navy. She was lent to France in 1946 and sold outright in 1951.

HMS GLORY in June 1945. Like COLOSSUS she completed before the end of hostilities and formed part of the 11th Aircraft Carrier Squadron under Rear Admiral CHJ Harcourt. She had CORSAIRS of 1831 Squadron and BARRACUDAS of 837 Squadron embarked. GLORY saw no action but did carry General BAH Sturdee of the Australian Army to accept the surrender of Japanese forces in New Britain during September 1945.

A CORSAIR crashes into the barrier of HMS COLOSSUS during flying operations shortly after World War 2. The aircraft is the personal machine of the Air Group Commander and has the Ship's crest on the tailplane. The markings are an odd mixture with East Indies pattern roundels on the fuselage and starboard wing and British Pacific Fleet roundel and bar markings on the port wing. The aircraft is painted in the midnight blue finish of aircraft delivered to the fleet direct from the USA unlike the sea grey/green finish of those delivered via the UK.

A FIREBRAND TF4 in the markings used by the Fleet Air Arm in the early post war years. FIREBRANDS were used as strike fighters with limited success until the turbo-prop WYVERN came to the end of its protracted development.

HMS ILLUSTRIOUS seen post war as a trials and training carrier. The aircraft on deck is a FIRE-BRAND. Some idea of the strength of the armoured flight deck can be gathered from the size of the supporting structure visible at the after end of the forward lift well.

The Royal Navy used MOSQUITOS extensively in the late 1940s. Some like this T3 were former RAF machines but some were built specifically for the Navy as strike aircraft. This machine served with 762 Squadron, the twin-engine conversion Unit based at RNAS CULDROSE in 1948/49. The aircraft has suffered a starboard engine fire, probably after a forced landing, which has been extinguished with foam. The salvage team have arrived and are making preparations to lift the aircraft in order to get the starboard undercarriage down. Note the lifting strops attached to the beam placed ready on the grass to the right of the picture.

The Landing Signals Officer (LSO) stood on a platform on the port after side of the flight deck, from where his signals could most easily be seen by approaching pilots. The windscreen forward of the platform is lowered.

Slats in the wind-screen that were broken or damaged could be replaced by sliding new ones into the frames. The slats made the raising or lowering of the screen possible even when there was a great deal of wind over the deck since one slat at a time could be moved.

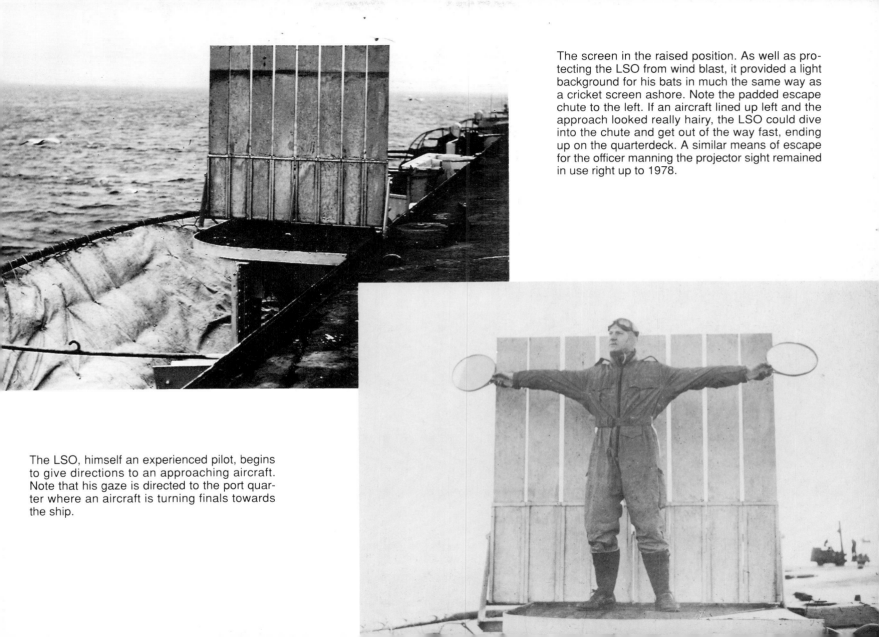

The screen in the raised position. As well as protecting the LSO from wind blast, it provided a light background for his bats in much the same way as a cricket screen ashore. Note the padded escape chute to the left. If an aircraft lined up left and the approach looked really hairy, the LSO could dive into the chute and get out of the way fast, ending up on the quarterdeck. A similar means of escape for the officer manning the projector sight remained in use right up to 1978.

The LSO, himself an experienced pilot, begins to give directions to an approaching aircraft. Note that his gaze is directed to the port quarter where an aircraft is turning finals towards the ship.

An early post-war shot of a FIREFLY FR1 landing on HMS TRIUMPH. The aircraft has taken a wire but pitched forward causing the propellers to peck the deck. The wire is firmly held by the arrester hook, so the aircraft is in no danger of somersaulting. The aircraft is from 827 Squadron which served in TRIUMPH whilst she was with the Mediterranean Fleet.

A FIREFLY FR1 going over the port side of a Light Fleet Carrier. The propellors have hit the spurn water on the deck edge and pieces of shattered blade are shooting in all directions.

This SEA HORNET F20 of 801 Squadron has lined up high and right. He is number two of a section of two fighters recovering onto HMS IMPLACABLE in 1948. The Squadron CO has already landed on and is parking forward.

The aircraft in the previous picture clipped the island with its wing and has crashed into IMPLA-CABLE's deck park forward striking the CO's aircraft which still has its engines running. The area where the two aircraft hit is beginning to burn. The partially folded aircraft forward is a FIREBRAND TF5.

A Sikorsky HOVERFLY fitted with floats being pushed onto the water at PORTLAND Naval Base. These American built aircraft were the first helicopters to enter squadron service with the Fleet Air Arm, equipping 771 Squadron at Portland in September 1945. Note the trolley arrangement under the floats used for moving the aircraft into and out of the water.

A SEA HORNET F20 seconds before taking a wire on HMS IMPLACABLE. The LSO has given the "CUT" signal and the aircraft is in a good landing atittude. Note how the arrester wires are kept off the deck by bowsprings, curved pieces of metal held up by vertical pistons. When flying is not in progress the pistons are lowered, bringing the bowsprings and thus the wires flat on the deck where they cause less obstruction to aircraft and vehicle movement.

Not what it seems! This is in fact an ex RAF HORNET PR2 used to test the barrier designed specifically for SEA HORNET operations. This one has worked well and has brought the aircraft to rest without causing any damage to the cockpit area. A special barrier had to be designed since, unlike a conventional piston engined naval aircraft, the SEA HORNET had no engine in front of the pilot to protect him from the barrier in use at that time. The trial nature of the operation explains the lack of any excitement or concern, and the shabby state of the aircraft which is a hack about to be written off.

Lt Cdr G R CALLINGHAM RN lands VR546, the prototype GANNET, on the trials carrier HMS ILLUSTRIOUS on 19 June 1950. This was the first time a turbo-prop aircraft had ever landed on a carrier, hence the LSO's close attention as the aircraft takes the cut. Note the windbreak in the folded down position and the padded escape chute.

A SEA VAMPIRE F21 carrying out an experimental landing on a rubber deck fitted to HMS WARRIOR in 1949. Whilst these aircraft had undercarriages, they were intended to prove the concept of landing undercarriageless aircraft on ships. These, it was felt, would be lighter and thus faster than their wheeled contemporaries. Whilst the concept might have had some theoretical merit, it was never to succeed because, once the aircraft had come to a stop on the rubber mat, it would have to be craned off and put on a trolley for movement. This was a very time consuming operation and would have made the use of more than 2 or 3 aircraft impossible. The sheer enormity of having to provide a rubber runway at every airfield in the world where naval aircraft might need to land would also have made the scheme an impossible one to implement.

SEA HORNET FR20s of 728 Squadron based at RNAS HAL FAR, MALTA GC. These are two of a batch of 5 SEA HORNETS allocated to the Squadron in 1952 for Fleet Requirements duties.

A SEA FURY FB11 – with a stork on its canopy. The aircraft is in Korean War recognition stripes and has 500lb bombs underwing outboard of the drop tanks. SEA FURIES were the standard single seat fighters of the Royal Navy from the late 1940s to the mid 1950s when they were replaced by the SEAHAWK. Operating from British and Australian light fleet carriers off Korea they flew in support of the Commonwealth troops ashore and proved themselves to be excellent ground attack aircraft.

A FIREFLY AS6 is lifted clear of the landing area after an accident on the flight deck of HMS EAGLE.

A FIREFLY FR4 of 817 Squadron about to be catapulted from HMAS SYDNEY during her tour of duty off KOREA in 1951. Note the automatic chocks raised from the deck to keep the aircraft in the correct position relative to the catapult and the holdback laying on deck under the aircraft's rudder. The holdback worked using a weak link; once the aircraft had run up to full power, the hydraulic catapult was fired and its force, acting through a wire strop, pulled the aircraft against the holdback. When the force was sufficient the weak link broke allowing the aircraft to accelerate away. Flight deck machinery such as catapults and wires were maintained by ships mechanical engineers who were identified by white surcoats with a black bar running vertically up them. They were familiarly known as "badgers" and two badgers can be seen in the group astern of the aircraft waiting to attach the holdback and launching strop. The planeguard helicopter is a USN S-51 DRAGONFLY on loan to the ship.

A Westland built SEAFIRE F15 of 1832 Squadron RNVR, based at RNAS CULHAM. The Squadron was reformed as a reserve unit at Culham in 1947 and operated a variety of SEAFIRES until they were replaced with SEA FURIES in 1951. This aircraft has started and two chockmen are awaiting the marshaller's signal to remove the chocks and let the pilot taxi forward for a brake check.

An immaculate FIREFLY FR5 is lowered onto the deck of a carrier during the Korean War. Replacement aircraft were ferried out to the operational carriers in HMS UNICORN and transferred by lighter during rest periods out of the combat zone. Seamen are seen working on a 32' cutter; the problem of "who does what" on a flight deck when no actual flying is in progress is an old one and there is no ideal solution. Aircraft maintenance and groundruns, sport, boat repairs, ship husbandry and the movement of stores all have to be given their due priority.

A FIREFLY FR5 of 810 Squadron joins the waiting pattern over HMS OCEAN with its hook down ready for recovery. A launch is in progress with a range of SEA FURIES forward being catapulted, whilst aft, two AVENGERS are running ready for a free take off. The planeguard DRAGONFLY is airborne to starboard.

A SEA FURY FB11 being ranged on the after lift of HMS GLORY. The lift driver is on the right with a white square stitched onto the back of his action working dress shirt. It is intended to show his tractor team number but countless "dhobey sessions" have left the number too faint to read. He has just let go of the operating bar that runs vertically down the lift wall and is about to reach for the brass lift operating handle to his right. He needs to be able to stop the lift in an instant if something goes wrong. Note the loose aircraft covers on the port wing. It is bad practice to leave loose items on the aircraft during a move. They could be caught by the wind and at best lost overboard; at worst they could strike another aircraft causing damage. The pilot in battledress is probably the Squadron Duty Officer keeping an eye on aircraft moves.

SEA FURY FB11s of 804 Squadron lined up on HMS THESEUS ready to be catapulted. FIREFLY FR 5s in the range behind them have not yet started. Catapult launching became the normal method toward the end of World War 2 since it allowed a larger number of aircraft to be ranged on deck and launched from a distance far shorter than that which would have been required for a free take off. A small carrier such as THESEUS could thus carry more aircraft by making use of a permanent deck park and could launch a large number in a single strike.

HMS TRIUMPH, 16 May 1952. A SEA FURY FB 11 has floated over the wires and then touched down main wheels first before crashing into the barrier in a nose-up attitude. Its momentum is sufficient for it to somersault onto its back.

The aircraft has come to rest upside down.

Once the risk of fire is over, the aircraft is dragged onto the forward lift and the crane is connected to strops wrapped around the after fuselage. The tail is then slowly lifted. Note the cautionary statement "A HOT ENGINE IS ALWAYS ON CONTACT" painted on the deep beam at the forward end of the lift structure.

Kept stable by a number of guide lines (and a considerable percentage of the Ship's Company) the aircraft is moved through the vertical. Once the tail wheel is on the deck the lift will be raised under the main wheels and the aircraft towed away for repairs. It says a lot for the strength of the airframe that it could take this sort of punishment and remain in one piece.

HMS OCEAN with a strike of SEA FURIES and FIREFLIES ranged and about to start up. Even this sizeable array of aircraft does not quite fully reflect the number that a light fleet carrier could launch for a single strike but it is close to it.